Magna Carta Libertatum of 1215

Arild Kolsrud

Copyright © 2019 Arild Kolsrud

All rights reserved.

ISBN: 9781797447735

CONTENTS

1. Prelude — 1
2. The council of 25 barons — 3
3. Councilors of the Magna Carta — 4
4. Magna Carta Libertatum of 1215 — 5
5. Sources — 17

1 PRELUDE

The Magna Carta Libertatum (Latin for "The Great Charter of the Liberties") is a charter of rights and liberties drafted by the Archbishop of Canterbury (Stephen Langton) and agreed to between King John of England and a group of rebel barons. It was signed and put in effect at Runnymede, near Windsor, on 15 June 1215. This charter, or document, was a turning point in human rights as it established the principle that everyone, including the king himself, is subject to the law of the land, and guarantees the rights of individuals, the right to justice and the right to a fair trial. It further established the right of the church to be free from governmental interference, the rights of all free citizens to own and inherit property and to be protected from excessive taxes.

Tension between King John and a number of Barons had been brewing for a while prior to the creation of the Magna Carta Libertatum. The territory of Normandy was taken away from King John by King Philip II of France in June 1204. This reduced the state income tax greatly, hence King John had to increase the tax collected on the remaining kingdom. When more taxes had to be raised after a failed military campaign to retake Normandy from King Philip II of France in the second half of 1214, a large number of British barons refused to pay the taxes. The barons had lost faith in King John being able to retake lost territory. In May 1215 forty barons renounced their respect and recognition of King John and marched with Scottish and French allies militarily on London as self-proclaimed "Army of God". This action led King John to organize peace talks with the rebel barons through Archbishop of Canterbury, Stephen Langton. Having Pope Innocent III on his side, King John exerted extra pressure on the rebel barons by using Stephen Langton to his advantage.

Stephen Langton's attempted mediation of peace between the king and the rebel barons resulted in the Magna Carta being drawn and signed on June 15, 1215 at Runnymede, near Windsor. The resulting charter went beyond addressing the complaints of the rebel barons, and formed a wider proposal of agreement for political reform focusing on free men but not serfs and other laborers bound by the feudal society. The charter promised further the protection of church rights, protection from illegal imprisonment, access to swift justice, new taxation only with consent of the barons themselves and limitations on scutage and other feudal payments. A special council of twenty-five barons would be created to monitor and ensure King John's adherence to the charter. In addition, the rebel army of the barons would surrender London, which they had captured a few weeks earlier.

Unfortunately, neither King John nor the rebel barons intended on keeping and adhere to the charter they signed. The rebel barons knew that King John would not accept the monitoring council of 25 barons and that he would challenge the legality of the signed charter. The rebel army was not demobilized nor was London surrendered back to the king. King John appealed to Pope Innocent III for help claiming the signed charter compromised the church's standing in England. The pope followed through on King John's request for help declaring the charter illegal. In addition to the denunciation of the charter, the pope excommunicated the rebel barons. The king's refusal to abide by the signed charter lead to the First Barons' War that lasted from the second half of 1215 to mid-1217.

2 THE COUNCIL OF 25 BARONS

The 25 Barons appointed under the Magna Carta's clause 61 were selected to monitor and ensure King John's compliance of the terms as well as his conduct. The opposition barons were afraid that King John would declare the Magna Carta as an infringement on his authority as soon as he left Runnymede where the charter was signed. The name of the barons selected for the council ensuring the compliance of the king to the charter were not listed in the charter itself as it an elected post and council participants could be changed and/or elected in the future. The barons that were initially selected for the council were all hardline opposition barons. The names of the 25 barons are listed alphabetically below:

1. William d'Aubigny, Lord of Belvoir
2. Hugh Bigod, heir to the Earldoms of Norfolk and Suffolk
3. Roger Bigod, Earl of Norfolk and Suffolk
4. Henry de Bohun, Earl of Hereford
5. Gilbert de Clare, heir to the earldom of Hertford
6. Richard de Clare, Earl of Hertford
7. John FitzRobert de Clavering, Lord of Warkworth Castle
8. Robert Fitzwalter, Baron of Little Dunmow
9. William de Forz, Earl of Albemarle
10. William Hardell, Mayor of the City of London
11. William of Huntingfield, Sheriff of Norfolk and Suffolk
12. John de Lacy, Constable of Chester and Lord of Pontefract Castle
13. William de Lanvallei, Lord of Walkern
14. Geoffrey de Mandeville, Earl of Essex and Gloucester
15. William Marshal junior, 2nd Earl of Pembroke
16. Roger de Montbegon, Lord of Hornby Castle, Lancashire
17. Richard de Montfichet
18. William de Mowbray, Lord of Axholme Castle
19. Richard de Percy
20. Robert de Ros, Baron of Helmsley
21. Geoffrey de Saye
22. Saer de Quincy, Earl of Winchester
23. William Malet, Baron of Curry Mallet, Somerset
24. Robert de Vere, Earl of Oxford
25. Eustace de Vesci, Lord of Alnwick Castle

3 COUNCILORS OF THE MAGNA CARTA

The beginning of the Magna Carta lists the individuals, loyal to the king himself, who had counselled King John on the peace treaty. There are a total of 27 individuals, members of the church and private individuals, and the names are listed below in the order they appear in the Magna Carta:

1. Stephen Langton, Archbishop of Canterbury and Cardinal
2. Henry de Loundres, Archbishop of Dublin
3. William of Sainte-Mère-Église, Bishop of London
4. Peter des Roches, Bishop of Winchester
5. Jocelin of Wells, Bishop of Bath and Glastonbury
6. Hugh of Wells, Bishop of Lincoln
7. Walter de Gray, Bishop of Worcester
8. William de Cornhill, Bishop of Coventry
9. Benedict of Sausetun, Bishop of Rochester
10. Pandulf Verraccio, subdeacon and papal legate to England
11. Eymeric, Master of the Knights Templar in England
12. William Marshal, Earl of Pembroke
13. William Longespée, Earl of Salisbury
14. William de Warenne, Earl of Surrey
15. William d'Aubigny, Earl of Arundel
16. Alan of Galloway, Constable of Scotland
17. Warin FitzGerold
18. Peter FitzHerbert
19. Hubert de Burgh, Seneschal of Poitou
20. Hugh de Neville
21. Matthew FitzHerbert
22. Thomas Basset
23. Alan Basset
24. Philip d'Aubigny
25. Robert of Ropsley
26. John Marshal
27. John FitzHugh

4 MAGNA CARTA LIBERTATUM OF 1215

JOHN, by the grace of God King of England, Lord of Ireland, Duke of Normandy and Aquitaine, and Count of Anjou, to his archbishops, bishops, abbots, earls, barons, justices, foresters, sheriffs, stewards, servants, and to all his officials and loyal subjects, Greeting.

KNOW THAT BEFORE GOD, for the health of our soul and those of our ancestors and heirs, to the honour of God, the exaltation of the holy Church, and the better ordering of our kingdom, at the advice of our reverend fathers Stephen, archbishop of Canterbury, primate of all England, and cardinal of the holy Roman Church, Henry archbishop of Dublin, William bishop of London, Peter bishop of Winchester, Jocelin bishop of Bath and Glastonbury, Hugh bishop of Lincoln, Walter bishop of Worcester, William bishop of Coventry, Benedict bishop of Rochester, Master Pandulf subdeacon and member of the papal household, Brother Aymeric master of the knighthood of the Temple in England, William Marshal earl of Pembroke, William earl of Salisbury, William earl of Warren, William earl of Arundel, Alan of Galloway constable of Scotland, Warin fitz Gerald, Peter fitz Herbert, Hubert de Burgh seneschal of Poitou, Hugh de Neville, Matthew fitz Herbert, Thomas Basset, Alan Basset, Philip Daubeny, Robert de Roppeley, John Marshal, John fitz Hugh, and other loyal subjects:

Clause 1:
FIRST, THAT WE HAVE GRANTED TO GOD, and by this present charter have confirmed for us and our heirs in perpetuity, that the English Church shall be free, and shall have its rights undiminished, and its liberties unimpaired. That we wish this so to be observed, appears from the fact that of our own free will, before the outbreak of the present dispute between us and our barons, we granted and confirmed by charter the freedom of the Church's elections - a right reckoned to be of the greatest necessity and importance to it - and caused this to be confirmed by Pope Innocent III. This freedom we shall observe ourselves, and desire to be observed in good faith by our heirs in perpetuity.

TO ALL FREE MEN OF OUR KINGDOM we have also granted, for us and our heirs forever, all the liberties written out below, to have and to keep for them and their heirs, of us and our heirs:

Clause 2:
If any earl, baron, or other person that holds lands directly of the

Crown, for military service, shall die, and at his death his heir shall be of full age and owe a 'relief', the heir shall have his inheritance on payment of the ancient scale of 'relief'. That is to say, the heir or heirs of an earl shall pay £100 for the entire earl's barony, the heir or heirs of a knight 100s. at most for the entire knight's 'fee', and any man that owes less shall pay less, in accordance with the ancient usage of 'fees'.

Clause 3:
But if the heir of such a person is under age and a ward, when he comes of age he shall have his inheritance without 'relief' or fine.

Clause 4:
The guardian of the land of an heir who is under age shall take from it only reasonable revenues, customary dues, and feudal services. He shall do this without destruction or damage to men or property. If we have given the guardianship of the land to a sheriff, or to any person answerable to us for the revenues, and he commits destruction or damage, we will exact compensation from him, and the land shall be entrusted to two worthy and prudent men of the same 'fee', who shall be answerable to us for the revenues, or to the person to whom we have assigned them. If we have given or sold to anyone the guardianship of such land, and he causes destruction or damage, he shall lose the guardianship of it, and it shall be handed over to two worthy and prudent men of the same 'fee', who shall be similarly answerable to us.

Clause 5:
For so long as a guardian has guardianship of such land, he shall maintain the houses, parks, fish preserves, ponds, mills, and everything else pertaining to it, from the revenues of the land itself. When the heir comes of age, he shall restore the whole land to him, stocked with plough teams and such implements of husbandry as the season demands and the revenues from the land can reasonably bear.

Clause 6:
Heirs may be given in marriage, but not to someone of lower social standing. Before a marriage takes place, it shall be made known to the heir's next-of-kin.

Clause 7:
At her husband's death, a widow may have her marriage portion and inheritance at once and without trouble. She shall pay nothing for her dower, marriage portion, or any inheritance that she and her husband held jointly on the day of his death. She may remain in her husband's house for

forty days after his death, and within this period her dower shall be assigned to her.

Clause 8:

No widow shall be compelled to marry, so long as she wishes to remain without a husband. But she must give security that she will not marry without royal consent, if she holds her lands of the Crown, or without the consent of whatever other lord she may hold them of.

Clause 9:

Neither we nor our officials will seize any land or rent in payment of a debt, so long as the debtor has movable goods sufficient to discharge the debt. A debtor's sureties shall not be distrained upon so long as the debtor himself can discharge his debt. If, for lack of means, the debtor is unable to discharge his debt, his sureties shall be answerable for it. If they so desire, they may have the debtor's lands and rents until they have received satisfaction for the debt that they paid for him, unless the debtor can show that he has settled his obligations to them.

Clause 10:

If anyone who has borrowed a sum of money from Jews dies before the debt has been repaid, his heir shall pay no interest on the debt for so long as he remains under age, irrespective of whom he holds his lands. If such a debt falls into the hands of the Crown, it will take nothing except the principal sum specified in the bond.

Clause 11:

If a man dies owing money to Jews, his wife may have her dower and pay nothing towards the debt from it. If he leaves children that are under age, their needs may also be provided for on a scale appropriate to the size of his holding of lands. The debt is to be paid out of the residue, reserving the service due to his feudal lords. Debts owed to persons other than Jews are to be dealt with similarly.

Clause 12:

No 'scutage' or 'aid' may be levied in our kingdom without its general consent, unless it is for the ransom of our person, to make our eldest son a knight, and (once) to marry our eldest daughter. For these purposes only a reasonable 'aid' may be levied. 'Aids' from the city of London are to be treated similarly.

Clause 13:

The city of London shall enjoy all its ancient liberties and free customs, both by land and by water. We also will and grant that all other cities, boroughs, towns, and ports shall enjoy all their liberties and free customs.

Clause 14:
To obtain the general consent of the realm for the assessment of an 'aid' - except in the three cases specified above - or a 'scutage', we will cause the archbishops, bishops, abbots, earls, and greater barons to be summoned individually by letter. To those who hold lands directly of us we will cause a general summons to be issued, through the sheriffs and other officials, to come together on a fixed day (of which at least forty days notice shall be given) and at a fixed place. In all letters of summons, the cause of the summons will be stated. When a summons has been issued, the business appointed for the day shall go forward in accordance with the resolution of those present, even if not all those who were summoned have appeared.

Clause 15:
In future we will allow no one to levy an 'aid' from his free men, except to ransom his person, to make his eldest son a knight, and (once) to marry his eldest daughter. For these purposes only a reasonable 'aid' may be levied.

Clause 16:
No man shall be forced to perform more service for a knight's 'fee', or other free holding of land, than is due from it.

Clause 17:
Ordinary lawsuits shall not follow the royal court around, but shall be held in a fixed place.

Clause 18:
Inquests of novel disseisin, mort d'ancestor, and darrein presentment shall be taken only in their proper county court. We ourselves, or in our absence abroad our chief justice, will send two justices to each county four times a year, and these justices, with four knights of the county elected by the county itself, shall hold the assizes in the county court, on the day and in the place where the court meets.

Clause 19:
If any assizes cannot be taken on the day of the county court, as many knights and freeholders shall afterwards remain behind, of those who have attended the court, as will suffice for the administration of justice, having regard to the volume of business to be done.

Clause 20:
For a trivial offence, a free man shall be fined only in proportion to the degree of his offence, and for a serious offence correspondingly, but not so heavily as to deprive him of his livelihood. In the same way, a merchant shall be spared his merchandise, and a villein the implements of his husbandry, if they fall upon the mercy of a royal court. None of these fines shall be imposed except by the assessment on oath of reputable men of the neighborhood.

Clause 21:
Earls and barons shall be fined only by their equals, and in proportion to the gravity of their offence.

Clause 22:
A fine imposed upon the lay property of a clerk in holy orders shall be assessed upon the same principles, without reference to the value of his ecclesiastical benefice.

Clause 23:
No town or person shall be forced to build bridges over rivers except those with an ancient obligation to do so.

Clause 24:
No sheriff, constable, coroners, or other royal officials are to hold lawsuits that should be held by the royal justices.

Clause 25:
Every county, hundred, wapentake, and tithing shall remain at its ancient rent, without increase, except the royal demesne manors.

Clause 26:
If at the death of a man who holds a lay 'fee' of the Crown, a sheriff or royal official produces royal letters patent of summons for a debt due to the Crown, it shall be lawful for them to seize and list movable goods found in the lay 'fee' of the dead man to the value of the debt, as assessed by worthy men. Nothing shall be removed until the whole debt is paid, when the residue shall be given over to the executors to carry out the dead man's will. If no debt is due to the Crown, all the movable goods shall be regarded as the property of the dead man, except the reasonable shares of his wife and children.

Clause 27:
If a free man dies intestate, his movable goods are to be distributed by

his next-of-kin and friends, under the supervision of the Church. The rights of his debtors are to be preserved.

Clause 28:
No constable or other royal official shall take corn or other movable goods from any man without immediate payment, unless the seller voluntarily offers postponement of this.

Clause 29:
No constable may compel a knight to pay money for castle-guard if the knight is willing to undertake the guard in person, or with reasonable excuse to supply some other fit man to do it. A knight taken or sent on military service shall be excused from castle-guard for the period of this service.

Clause 30:
No sheriff, royal official, or other person shall take horses or carts for transport from any free man, without his consent.

Clause 31:
Neither we nor any royal official will take wood for our castle, or for any other purpose, without the consent of the owner.

Clause 32:
We will not keep the lands of people convicted of felony in our hand for longer than a year and a day, after which they shall be returned to the lords of the 'fees' concerned.

Clause 33:
All fish-weirs shall be removed from the Thames, the Medway, and throughout the whole of England, except on the sea coast.

Clause 34:
The writ called precipe shall not in future be issued to anyone in respect of any holding of land, if a free man could thereby be deprived of the right of trial in his own lord's court.

Clause 35:
There shall be standard measures of wine, ale, and corn (the London quarter), throughout the kingdom. There shall also be a standard width of dyed cloth, russet, and haberject, namely two ells within the selvedges. Weights are to be standardized similarly.

Clause 36:

In future nothing shall be paid or accepted for the issue of a writ of inquisition of life or limbs. It shall be given gratis, and not refused.

Clause 37:

If a man holds land of the Crown by 'fee-farm', 'socage', or 'burgage', and also holds land of someone else for knight's service, we will not have guardianship of his heir, nor of the land that belongs to the other person's 'fee', by virtue of the 'fee-farm', 'socage', or 'burgage', unless the 'fee-farm' owes knight's service. We will not have the guardianship of a man's heir, or of land that he holds of someone else, by reason of any small property that he may hold of the Crown for a service of knives, arrows, or the like.

Clause 38:

In future no official shall place a man on trial upon his own unsupported statement, without producing credible witnesses to the truth of it.

Clause 39:

No free man shall be seized or imprisoned, or stripped of his rights or possessions, or outlawed or exiled, or deprived of his standing in any way, nor will we proceed with force against him, or send others to do so, except by the lawful judgment of his equals or by the law of the land.

Clause 40:

To no one will we sell, to no one deny or delay right or justice.

Clause 41:

All merchants may enter or leave England unharmed and without fear, and may stay or travel within it, by land or water, for purposes of trade, free from all illegal exactions, in accordance with ancient and lawful customs. This, however, does not apply in time of war to merchants from a country that is at war with us. Any such merchants found in our country at the outbreak of war shall be detained without injury to their persons or property, until we or our chief justice have discovered how our own merchants are being treated in the country at war with us. If our own merchants are safe they shall be safe too.

Clause 42:

In future it shall be lawful for any man to leave and return to our kingdom unharmed and without fear, by land or water, preserving his allegiance to us, except in time of war, for some short period, for the common benefit of the realm. People that have been imprisoned or outlawed in accordance with the law of the land, people from a country that is at war with us, and merchants - who shall be dealt with as stated above - are excepted from this provision.

Clause 43:
If a man holds lands of any 'escheat' such as the 'honour' of Wallingford, Nottingham, Boulogne, Lancaster, or of other 'escheats' in our hand that are baronies, at his death his heir shall give us only the 'relief' and service that he would have made to the baron, had the barony been in the baron's hand. We will hold the 'escheat' in the same manner as the baron held it.

Clause 44:
People who live outside the forest need not in future appear before the royal justices of the forest in answer to general summonses, unless they are actually involved in proceedings or are sureties for someone who has been seized for a forest offence.

Clause 45:
We will appoint as justices, constables, sheriffs, or other officials, only men that know the law of the realm and are minded to keep it well.

Clause 46:
All barons who have founded abbeys, and have charters of English kings or ancient tenure as evidence of this, may have guardianship of them when there is no abbot, as is their due.

Clause 47:
All forests that have been created in our reign shall at once be disafforested. River-banks that have been enclosed in our reign shall be treated similarly.

Clause 48:
All evil customs relating to forests and warrens, foresters, warreners, sheriffs and their servants, or river-banks and their wardens, are at once to be investigated in every county by twelve sworn knights of the county, and within forty days of their enquiry the evil customs are to be abolished completely and irrevocably. But we, or our chief justice if we are not in England, are first to be informed.

Clause 49:
We will at once return all hostages and charters delivered up to us by Englishmen as security for peace or for loyal service.

Clause 50:

We will remove completely from their offices the kinsmen of Gerard de Athée, and in future they shall hold no offices in England. The people in question are Engelard de Cigogné, Peter, Guy, and Andrew de Chanceaux, Guy de Cigogné, Geoffrey de Martigny and his brothers, Philip Marc and his brothers, with Geoffrey his nephew, and all their followers.

Clause 51:

As soon as peace is restored, we will remove from the kingdom all the foreign knights, bowmen, their attendants, and the mercenaries that have come to it, to its harm, with horses and arms.

Clause 52:

To any man whom we have deprived or dispossessed of lands, castles, liberties, or rights, without the lawful judgment of his equals, we will at once restore these. In cases of dispute the matter shall be resolved by the judgment of the twenty-five barons referred to below in the clause for securing the peace (section 61). In cases, however, where a man was deprived or dispossessed of something without the lawful judgment of his equals by our father King Henry or our brother King Richard, and it remains in our hands or is held by others under our warranty, we shall have respite for the period commonly allowed to Crusaders, unless a lawsuit had been begun, or an enquiry had been made at our order, before we took the Cross as a Crusader. On our return from the Crusade, or if we abandon it, we will at once render justice in full.

Clause 53:

We shall have similar respite in rendering justice in connection with forests that are to be disafforested, or to remain forests, when these were first afforested by our father Henry or our brother Richard; with the guardianship of lands in another person's 'fee', when we have hitherto had this by virtue of a 'fee' held of us for knight's service by a third party; and with abbeys founded in another person's 'fee', in which the lord of the 'fee' claims to own a right. On our return from the Crusade, or if we abandon it, we will at once do full justice to complaints about these matters.

Clause 54:

No one shall be arrested or imprisoned on the appeal of a woman for the death of any person except her husband.

Clause 55:

All fines that have been given to us unjustly and against the law of the land, and all fines that we have exacted unjustly, shall be entirely remitted or the matter decided by a majority judgment of the twenty-five barons referred to below in the clause for securing the peace (§61) together with Stephen, archbishop of Canterbury, if he can be present, and such others as he wishes to bring with him. If the archbishop cannot be present, proceedings shall continue without him, provided that if any of the twenty-five barons has been involved in a similar suit himself, his judgment shall be set aside, and someone else chosen and sworn in his place, as a substitute for the single occasion, by the rest of the twenty-five.

Clause 56:

If we have deprived or dispossessed any Welshmen of land, liberties, or anything else in England or in Wales, without the lawful judgment of their equals, these are at once to be returned to them. A dispute on this point shall be determined in the Marches by the judgment of equals. English law shall apply to holdings of land in England, Welsh law to those in Wales, and the law of the Marches to those in the Marches. The Welsh shall treat us and ours in the same way.

Clause 57:

In cases where a Welshman was deprived or dispossessed of anything, without the lawful judgment of his equals, by our father King Henry or our brother King Richard, and it remains in our hands or is held by others under our warranty, we shall have respite for the period commonly allowed to Crusaders, unless a lawsuit had been begun, or an enquiry had been made at our order, before we took the Cross as a Crusader. But on our return from the Crusade, or if we abandon it, we will at once do full justice according to the laws of Wales and the said regions.

Clause 58:

We will at once return the son of Llywelyn, all Welsh hostages, and the charters delivered to us as security for the peace.

Clause 59:

With regard to the return of the sisters and hostages of Alexander, king of Scotland, his liberties and his rights, we will treat him in the same way as our other barons of England, unless it appears from the charters that we hold from his father William, formerly king of Scotland, that he should be treated otherwise. This matter shall be resolved by the judgment of his equals in our court.

Clause 60:

All these customs and liberties that we have granted shall be observed in our kingdom in so far as concerns our own relations with our subjects. Let all men of our kingdom, whether clergy or laymen, observe them similarly in their relations with their own men.

Clause 61:

SINCE WE HAVE GRANTED ALL THESE THINGS for God, for the better ordering of our kingdom, and to allay the discord that has arisen between us and our barons, and since we desire that they shall be enjoyed in their entirety, with lasting strength, for ever, we give and grant to the barons the following security:

The barons shall elect twenty-five of their number to keep, and cause to be observed with all their might, the peace and liberties granted and confirmed to them by this charter.

If we, our chief justice, our officials, or any of our servants offend in any respect against any man, or transgress any of the articles of the peace or of this security, and the offence is made known to four of the said twenty-five barons, they shall come to us – or in our absence from the kingdom to the chief justice – to declare it and claim immediate redress. If we, or in our absence abroad the chief justice, make no redress within forty days, reckoning from the day on which the offence was declared to us or to him, the four barons shall refer the matter to the rest of the twenty-five barons, who may distrain upon and assail us in every way possible, with the support of the whole community of the land, by seizing our castles, lands, possessions, or anything else saving only our own person and those of the queen and our children, until they have secured such redress as they have determined upon. Having secured the redress, they may then resume their normal obedience to us.

Any man who so desires may take an oath to obey the commands of the twenty-five barons for the achievement of these ends, and to join with them in assailing us to the utmost of his power. We give public and free permission to take this oath to any man who so desires, and at no time will we prohibit any man from taking it. Indeed, we will compel any of our subjects who are unwilling to take it to swear it at our command.

If one of the twenty-five barons dies or leaves the country, or is prevented in any other way from discharging his duties, the rest of them shall choose another baron in his place, at their discretion, who shall be duly sworn in as they were.

In the event of disagreement among the twenty-five barons on any matter referred to them for decision, the verdict of the majority present shall have the same validity as a unanimous verdict of the whole twenty-five, whether these were all present or some of those summoned were unwilling or unable to appear.

The twenty-five barons shall swear to obey all the above articles faithfully, and shall cause them to be obeyed by others to the best of their power.

We will not seek to procure from anyone, either by our own efforts or those of a third party, anything by which any part of these concessions or liberties might be revoked or diminished. Should such a thing be procured, it shall be null and void and we will at no time make use of it, either ourselves or through a third party.

Clause 62:

We have remitted and pardoned fully to all men any ill-will, hurt, or grudges that have arisen between us and our subjects, whether clergy or laymen, since the beginning of the dispute. We have in addition remitted fully, and for our own part have also pardoned, to all clergy and laymen any offences committed as a result of the said dispute between Easter in the sixteenth year of our reign (i.e. 1215) and the restoration of peace.

In addition we have caused letters patent to be made for the barons, bearing witness to this security and to the concessions set out above, over the seals of Stephen archbishop of Canterbury, Henry archbishop of Dublin, the other bishops named above, and Master Pandulf.

Clause 63:

IT IS ACCORDINGLY OUR WISH AND COMMAND that the English Church shall be free, and that men in our kingdom shall have and keep all these liberties, rights, and concessions, well and peaceably in their fullness and entirety for them and their heirs, of us and our heirs, in all things and all places for ever.

Both we and the barons have sworn that all this shall be observed in good faith and without deceit. Witness the abovementioned people and many others.

Given by our hand in the meadow that is called Runnymede, between Windsor and Staines, on the fifteenth day of June in the seventeenth year of our reign (i.e. 1215: the new regnal year began on 28 May).

The English translation of the Magna Carta Libertatum was obtained via Creative Commons License from https://www.bl.uk/magna-carta/articles/magna-carta-english-translation

5 SOURCES

Wells, H.G. The Outline of History. Garden City, NY: Garden City Publishing Company Inc., 1931, 1255 pp.

DeVos, J.E. Fifteen hundred years of Europe. Chicago, IL: The O'Donnell Press, 1924, 562 pp.

First Barons' War. (n.d.). Retrieved from https://en.wikipedia.org/

Magna Carta. (n.d.). Retrieved from https://en.wikipedia.org/

English translation of Magna Carta. 2014, July 28. Retrieved from https://www.bl.uk

The 25 Barons of Magna Carta. (n.d.). Retrieved from https://magnacarta800th.com

Arild Kolsrud

Magna Carta Libertatum of 1215

www.ingramcontent.com/pod-product-compliance
Lightning Source LLC
Chambersburg PA
CBHW071205220526
45468CB00003B/1166